NOTE T

Apologetics Press is a non-profit organization dedicated to the defense of New Testament Christianity. For over a quarter of a century, we have provided faith-building materials for adults. We also have produced numerous materials (like *Discovery* magazine, our *Explorer Series*, and various books) for young people in third grade through high school. We now are pleased to present a new series of books for even younger children.

The Apologetics Press Early Reader Series is a set of books aimed at children in kindergarten through second grade. Depending on the age of your children, this series is flexible enough to allow parents to read to their children, read along with their children, or they can listen while their children read aloud to them.

The books in this series are filled with beautiful full-color pictures and wonderful information about God, His creation, and His Word. These books are written on a level that early readers will enjoy, while drawing them closer to their Creator.

We hope you enjoy using the Apologetics Press Early Reader Series to encourage your children to read, while at the same time helping them learn about God and His creation.

1

God Made Dinosaurs

by Brad Harrub

Copyright © 2005
Apologetics Press

ISBN-10: 0-932859-71-2

ISBN-13: 978-0-932859-71-6

Library of Congress: 2005926994

Printed in China

God Made Dinosaurs

by Brad Harrub

Distributed by
CREATION SCIENCE ASSOCIATION
OF BRITISH COLUMBIA
www.creationbc.org
604-535-0019

God created one group of animals called dinosaurs.

They came in all
shapes and sizes.

Some dinosaurs   wer

very $B I G$;

much bigger
than elephants
we see today.

While others
were little,
about the size
of a large dog.

Some dinosaurs liked to eat leaves from the treetops.

Meat-eating
dinosaurs
also roamed
the planet.

But all dinosaurs
were made by God.

Some
of
these
animals
had very
long
necks.

Others had very
short necks.

Some had
mouths shaped
like a parrot.

Other dinosaurs
had mouths full
of sharp teeth!

God covered some dinosaurs with strong plates.

God covered other
dinosaurs with
spikes for
protection.

We believe that many dinosaurs traveled in large groups or herds.

Certain dinosaurs
had giant lumps
on their heads.

Some dinosaurs had
giant horns
coming
from their
heads.

Look at the big claws on this dinosaur's feet.

Humans once lived with these amazing animals.

Imagine having a dinosaur as a pet!

The Bible tells us
God created all
land-living animals
on the sixth day of
Creation, even dinosaurs.

We have
found fossils
of dinosaurs
all over the
world.

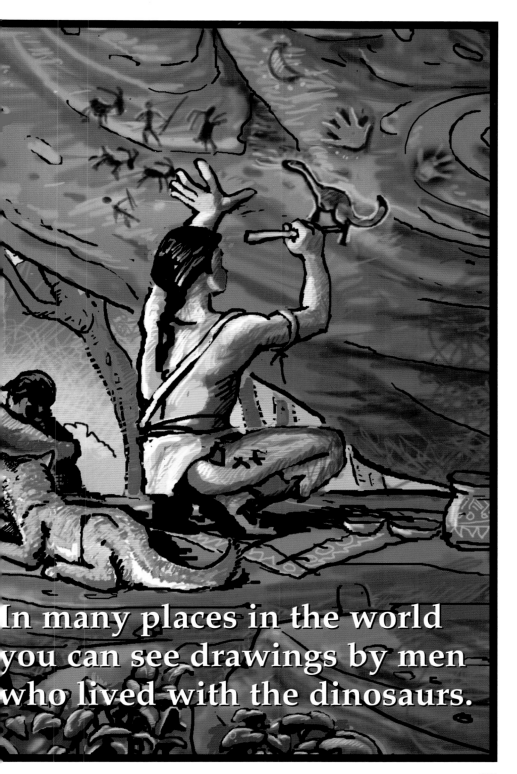

In many places in the world you can see drawings by men who lived with the dinosaurs.

Wouldn't it have been gre
window and see a dinosau

o look out of your bedroom
unning through your yard?

By learning about dinosaurs, we can learn about the God Who created them.